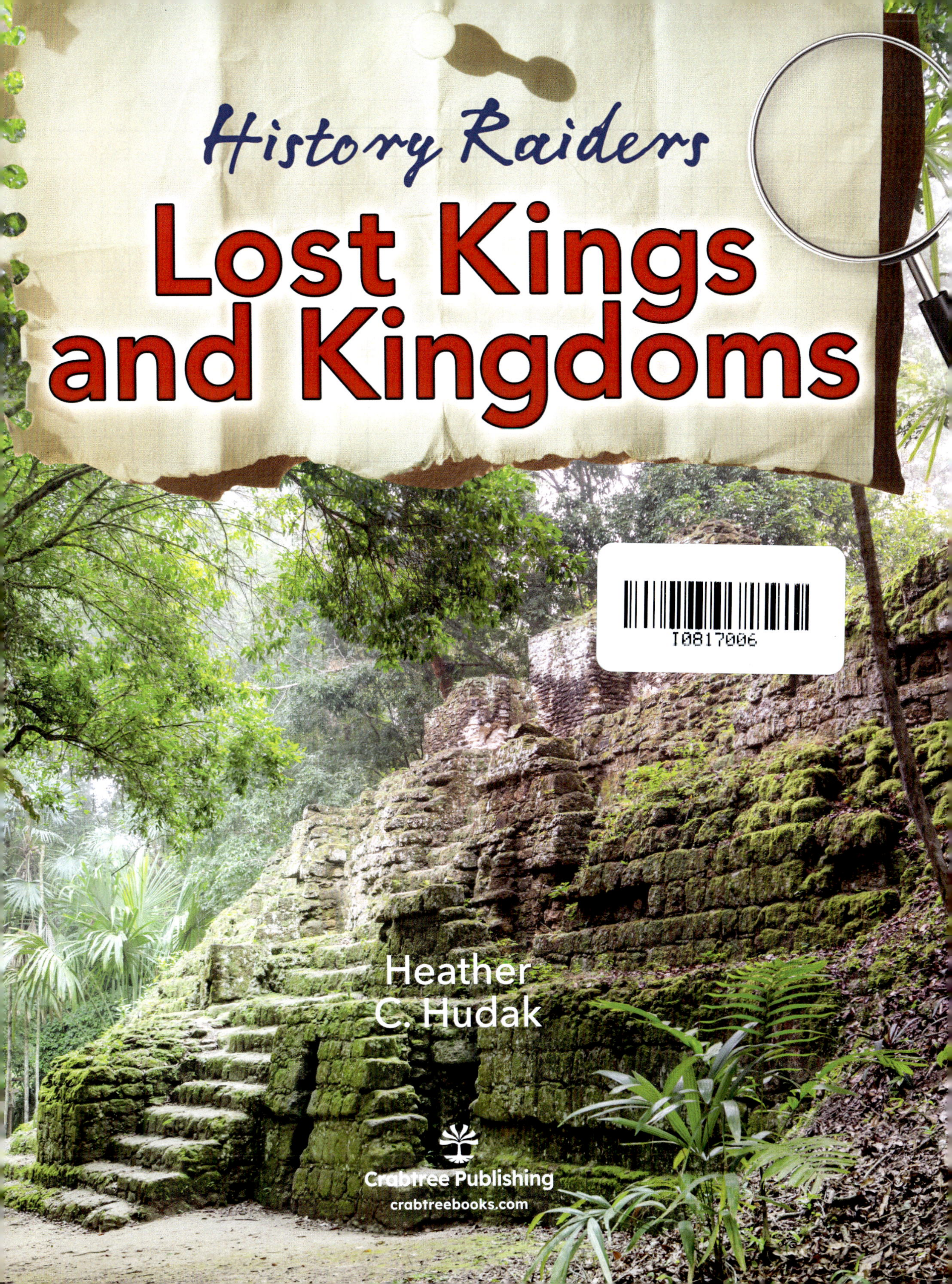

History Raiders

Lost Kings and Kingdoms

Heather C. Hudak

Crabtree Publishing
crabtreebooks.com

Crabtree Publishing

crabtreebooks.com 800-387-7650

 In Canada: We acknowledge the financial support of the Government of Canada through the Canada Book Fund for our publishing activities.

Author: Heather C. Hudak
Editors: Sarah Eason, Jennifer Sanderson, and Janine Deschenes
Proofreader and indexer: Tracey Kelly
Proofreader: Crystal Sikkens
Editorial director: Kathy Middleton
Design: Jessica Moon
Cover design: Katherine Kantor
Photo research: Rachel Blount
Production manager: Candice Campbell
Prepress technician: Katherine Kantor
Consultant: Rupert Matthews
Written, developed, and produced by Calcium

Hardcover 978-1-4271-5105-6
Paperback 978-1-4271-5111-7
Ebook (pdf) 978-1-4271-5117-9

Printed in the U.S.A./082025/CP20250811

Library and Archives Canada Cataloguing in Publication
Title: Lost kings and kingdoms / Heather C. Hudak.
Names: Hudak, Heather C., 1975- author.
Description: Series statement: History raiders | Includes bibliographical references and index.
Identifiers: Canadiana (print) 20210192577 | Canadiana (ebook) 20210192585 | ISBN 9781427151056 (hardcover) | ISBN 9781427151117 (softcover) | ISBN 9781427151179 (HTML) | ISBN 9781427151230 (EPUB)
Subjects: LCSH: Extinct cities—Juvenile literature. | LCSH: Civilization, Ancient—Juvenile literature. | LCSH: Archaeology—Juvenile literature.
Classification: LCC CC176 .H83 2022 | DDC j930.1—dc23

Published in Canada
Crabtree Publishing
616 Welland Avenue
St. Catharines, Ontario
L2M 5V6

Published in the United States
Crabtree Publishing
347 Fifth Avenue
Suite 1402-145
New York, NY 10016

Photo Credits:
t=Top, c=Center, b=Bottom, l= Left, r=Right

Cover: PHGCOM, Wikimedia Commons: coins bottom center; Rijksmuseum, Wikimedia Commons: bottom right; All other images by Shutterstock.
Inside: Jessica Moon: p. 20 cl; Shutterstock: Alexander P: p. 8 cl; Juan Aunion: p. 23c; Philip Bird LRPS CPAGB: p. 5; Bonoc: p. 6; Jennifer Cockram: p. 8 tl; Cherkashin Denis: p. 25; Digital Bazaar: p. 12 cl; Digital Storm: p. 3 & throughout; Fotokvadrat: p. 7; Jeffrey M. Frank: p. 21, 29 tr; Matt Gush: p. 16 tl; Russ Heinl: p. 19; Milje Ivan: p. 23r, 24 tl; Vladislav T. Jirousek: p. 4; Muellek Josef: p. 11; eck P. Kent: p. 18; Morphart Creation: p. 24 cl; Pander bear: p. 20; Gary Perkin: p. 9, 28 bl; Rocksweeper: p. 27; RozenskiP: p. 20 tl; Alexey Stiop: p 12; Sunsinger: p. 12 tl; Barna Tanko: p. 15; VarnaK: pp. 14, 29 bl; Vlada Young: p. 16 cl; Zehmaria84: p. 10; Wikimedia Commons: The Charles Machine Works: p. 26; Ángel M. Felicísimo (www.flickr.com/people/8146925@N08) from Mérida, España: p. 22; Glysiak: p. 16

Library of Congress Cataloging-in-Publication Data
Names: Hudak, Heather C., 1975- author.
Title: Lost kings and kingdoms / Heather C. Hudak.
Description: New York, NY : Crabtree Publishing Company, [2022] | Series: History raiders | Includes index.
Identifiers: LCCN 2021016640 (print) | LCCN 2021016641 (ebook) | ISBN 9781427151056 (hardcover) | ISBN 9781427151117 (paperback) | ISBN 9781427151179 (ebook) | ISBN 9781427151230 (epub)
Subjects: LCSH: Extinct cities--Juvenile literature. | Kings and rulers--Juvenile literature. | Civilization, Ancient--Juvenile literature. | Archaeology--Juvenile literature.
Classification: LCC CC176 .H83 2022 (print) | LCC CC176 (ebook) | DDC 930.1--dc23
LC record available at https://lccn.loc.gov/2021016640
LC ebook record available at https://lccn.loc.gov/2021016641

CONTENTS

HIDDEN KINGDOMS

For centuries, stories of kings and queens ruling over vast kingdoms have captured people's imaginations. Perhaps most fascinating of all are the stories of kingdoms and rulers that seem to have vanished.

Lost and Found

Archaeologists have discovered some lost kingdoms by finding their ruined buildings. Some were buried deep within the forests of Asia and the Americas. Others lay in ruins across European landscapes. Each building has played a part in shaping **historians**' knowledge of the **culture** and **civilizations** of the people who lived there. Today, many more hidden kingdoms are being discovered, thanks to modern-day archaeology. People are now able to journey through the past to learn about lost kingdoms and rulers, and uncover their ancient mysteries.

Tikal in Guatemala is the ruin of an ancient Mayan city. Many such cities of South America were hidden beneath jungles for thousands of years until they were discovered in the mid-1800s. They raised questions that historians are still trying to answer.

Boudicca was the powerful leader of a Celtic **tribe** in England known as the Iceni. She seems to have disappeared after a great battle with the Romans.

Explore History

In this book, we will journey across the world to discover fascinating lost rulers and kingdoms. As we do so, we will examine questions raised by these cases and gather **evidence** to try to answer them.

History Raider!

Hey! I'm Madison Maverick. I'm an explorer. I also like to think of myself as a history raider—a person who stops at nothing to find answers about the past. Come with me on my journeys to solve past mysteries and answer questions about history. Read my field notes on the History Raider pages and boxes. Then, jot down evidence to help solve each mystery.

LONG-LOST KINGS

Countless kingdoms formed across Europe after the Roman Empire **began to fall in 476 C.E. Many have been long forgotten or lost until now. Today, archaeologists and historians are digging into this history. They are learning more about** medieval **kingdoms and their fascinating rulers.**

Fighters Lost Forever

Some of the most fascinating medieval kingdoms were in Britain. It was home to warring tribes that often fought each other, as well as invading forces from other countries and regions. For example, the Picts lived in the far north of Britain. They were fierce and fought to the death to protect their land. During the Roman occupation of England (43 to 410 C.E.), the emperor Hadrian ordered a wall to be built. This giant stone **fortification** was named Hadrian's Wall. Hadrian thought it would keep the Picts out of the lands to the south.

These are some of the **remains** of Hadrian's Wall, which stretches for miles across England.

Britain's Most Mysterious King

Several early writings dating back as far as the 400s C.E. mention a great warrior named Arthur. They say he led the Britons in many battles. For years, historians have wondered if this warrior was actually the legendary King Arthur. They have been trying to trace the warrior's life to King Arthur and his great Camelot castle.

Stories tell of a wealthy city surrounded by beautiful forests and meadows. There, knights would often hold fighting competitions called tournaments. Camelot was also home to King Arthur's famous Round Table, which had room to seat 150 knights. Everyone who sat at the table was treated as an equal. Despite the many tales about King Arthur, there is little evidence of his actual existence, including what happened to him. He is one of history's greatest mysteries.

No one knows for sure what King Arthur looked like—or even if he existed. If he did exist, he may have been a powerful chieftain or the leader of a great tribe.

History Raider!

When I learned of King Arthur and his famous castle, I had to find out more. Was he really a great warrior, or does he exist only in stories? Where was Camelot? And if King Arthur really existed, what happened to him? I had to investigate...

History Raider!

Britain's Lost King

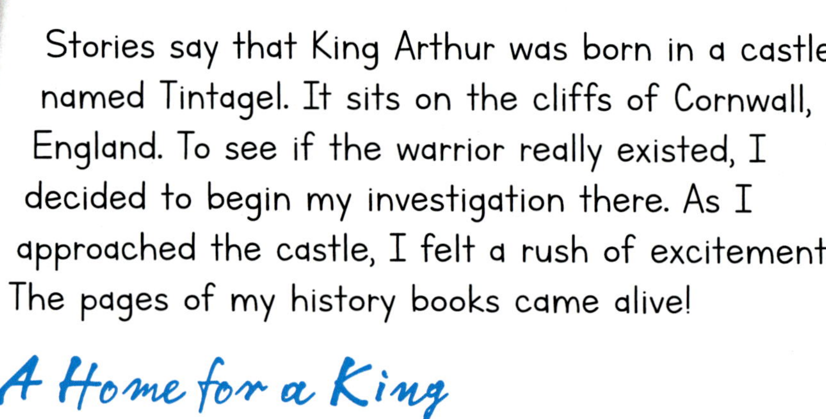

Stories say that King Arthur was born in a castle named Tintagel. It sits on the cliffs of Cornwall, England. To see if the warrior really existed, I decided to begin my investigation there. As I approached the castle, I felt a rush of excitement. The pages of my history books came alive!

A Home for a King

Walking across the castle grounds, I learned that people first lived in the area from the 400s to 600s C.E. I met some historians who were **excavating** the grounds. They had discovered that amazing stone buildings once sat right on the edge of the cliff. The team found the remains of magnificent bowls and cups dating back more than 1,000 years. They said the **artifacts** were a sign that very wealthy people and even kings had once lived there. Could King Arthur have been one of them?

The Road to Camelot

No one knows the exact site of Camelot. However, Caerleon in Wales is one of the places where people think that King Arthur may have built his castle. I headed there next. As I walked around the ancient site, I was struck by the **amphitheater**. I could see how it might have inspired stories of King Arthur's famous Round Table.

Rest in Peace

According to stories, King Arthur died after being wounded in battle in around 542 C.E. Many historians believe he was buried at a place called Avalon. This may have been the town now known as Glastonbury. I went there next to find out more. In 1191, **monks** claimed to have found King Arthur and his wife Guinevere buried at the ruins of Glastonbury **Abbey**. But some people believe their claim may have been a trick to draw tourists there. A fire had damaged the abbey, and the monks needed money from tourism to rebuild it. In the mid-1500s, the abbey, the **tomb**, and any evidence of King Arthur and his wife were destroyed. All I saw was a sign marking where the tomb had supposedly been. I guess I'll never know for sure if King Arthur and his wife were buried at Glastonbury.

This sculpture of King Arthur stands at Tintagel Castle in England.

Finding Answers

I still can't stop thinking about the story of King Arthur. Did you find evidence from my field notes that could help solve the mystery? Turn to pages 28–29 to learn if your findings match mine.

EMPIRES OF THE EAST

Archaeologists have unearthed evidence of ancient kingdoms all over Asia. Many were hidden from sight for hundreds of years. They were buried deep beneath the earth or thick forest cover. These exciting finds are helping us learn more about the long-lost rulers of Asia.

Cambodia's Hidden Treasure

One of the most fascinating of all ancient Asian kingdoms is the Khmer Empire. It began in 802 C.E. and lasted until 1431 C.E. The Khmer Empire stretched across most of present-day Cambodia. It also covered large parts of Thailand, Laos, and southern Vietnam. Khmer kings ruled the land from the royal city of Angkor. This sits near what is now known as Siem Reap, in Cambodia.

Jungle vines have grown over the ruins of Angkor.

Ancient Architects

The Khmer were known for their incredible building skills. They built massive temples and systems to water their crops. They also created a vast network of roadways and bridges. But all that remains of Angkor today are badly damaged stone temples. Wooden structures, such as homes and palaces, have long since rotted away. Many other artifacts have been hidden by jungle overgrowth. To this day, remains of the vast empire still lie hidden beneath the ground, just waiting for archaeologists to discover them!

Lost History

The Khmer rulers could read and write, yet no books or documents from the Khmer Empire exist today. They were probably written on palm leaves that rotted away over time. All that historians know about the empire comes from studies of ancient ruins and artifacts.

Ancient Khmer carvings cover the temple walls at Angkor Thom. This one shows soldiers marching into battle, while the commander rides on an elephant.

Swallowed by the Jungle

In 1860, French explorer Henri Mouhot hacked his way through the thick jungle around Angkor. As he did so, he stumbled across the giant blocks of carved stone that make up the magnificent Angkor Wat. This is a set of buildings that make up a Buddhist temple within the great and sprawling capital of Angkor. The story is that Mouhot had discovered the long-lost capital of the Khmer Empire. He said it had been hidden in the jungle for thousands of years.

History Raider!

After looking at pictures of Angkor Wat, I was puzzled. Why did the images I looked at show so many Hindu statues when the temple was used by Buddhists? Mouhot said the temple had been built 2,000 years ago, but was that true? Why had a once-great capital fallen into ruin?

History Raider!

Temple Lost in Time

I arrived at Angkor Wat at 5 a.m. to watch the Sun rise over the temple. Had Khmer kings once gazed at the Sun from this same spot? I was excited to see what ancient secrets I would uncover at the temple.

Hindu, Not Buddhist

As I wandered around, I traced my fingers over a statue of a Hindu god and stared at the Hindu images covering the walls of the temple. As my fingers lingered there, I still couldn't understand why so many Hindu artifacts were at a temple used by Buddhists. Then, I met a Buddhist monk who explained that the temple had been built by Hindus! The Buddhist monks had simply taken over the temple in 1177.

Angkor Wat was the largest religious area ever built. It spreads out over 500 acres (202 hectares).

Not so Long Ago

Next, the monk told me that Angkor Wat had been built in the early 12th century. This was way off Mouhot's guess that it had been built 2,000 years earlier! The monk then said that Mouhot did not discover Angkor Wat at all! He was just one of the first Europeans to visit it. Locals had always known about the temple and had used it as a place of worship for centuries!

Destroyed by an Enemy?

I still wanted to learn what had caused Angkor to fall into ruin. Everything I had read said that it had been attacked in 1431, and this had caused the collapse of the Khmer Empire. I was puzzled once more. It seemed very strange that an empire as great and mighty as Khmer had been so easily defeated. Determined to dig deeper, I spoke with an archaeologist who studied soil samples at the site. He had a different idea about what had happened. He claimed that heavy rains after a time of **drought** may have caused the city to crumble. Perhaps the temple and much of the great city had been washed away rather than destroyed by an enemy. Nevertheless, it seemed like a sad end to what had once been such a mighty kingdom.

Finding Answers

Wow! Angkor Wat was incredible. I have recorded all the evidence I could about this mysterious place. Turn to pages 28–29 to learn if your findings match mine!

LOST IN LATIN AMERICA

Dozens of ancient cultures once spread across Latin America**. Tales of golden cities with huge pyramids and beautiful palaces have long enchanted people worldwide. But many early kingdoms were taken over by other civilizations. Afterward, their remains were hidden, forgotten, and untouched for centuries.**

Lost City of the Inca

High atop the Andes Mountains 50 miles (80 km) outside Cuzco, Peru, are the ruins of an incredible Inca city. It is known as Machu Picchu. Only locals knew of Machu Picchu's existence until 1911, when an American archaeologist came across the site. There is no record of how or when the Inca built Machu Picchu or what purpose it served. Archaeologists believe it may have been a religious site or a royal vacation home for the Inca emperor. Skilled craftspeople may have been brought in from across the land to work at Machu Picchu. Researchers are studying **DNA** of skeletons found at the site to help prove this idea. Still, many secrets remain hidden in the ancient ruins.

No one knows why Machu Picchu was abandoned in the early 1500s. It may have been due to disease or lack of water.

Moving into Mexico

From about 1600 to 350 B.C.E., another mysterious civilization called the Olmec thrived in Latin America. It was found along the Gulf of Mexico in present-day Veracruz and Tabasco, Mexico. The Olmec civilization was the first great culture of **Mesoamerica**, but after about 2,000 years, it disappeared. Very few traces of the Olmec culture remain today. Much of what we know comes from studying its artwork and other artifacts. Some of the most notable pieces include lifelike heads carved from massive stones. Still, we know very little about how the Olmec lived or why their civilization came to an end. What happened to them remains one of history's great unexplained mysteries.

The Olmec built large stone tombs for their dead, like this one.

History Raider!

When I came across a website about a mysterious giant stone head a farmer had found in a Mexican forest in the mid-1800s, I couldn't help but wonder how it got there. Archaeologists believe the head was left by the Olmec, but I wondered how and why they'd made this giant object. And what could this artifact teach us about the Olmec? I had to learn more.

History Raider!

Losing Their Heads

I stared out the window as my plane touched down in Veracruz, Mexico. I was excited to start my investigation at the place where the first giant Olmec head was rediscovered.

Heads Up

It was a two-and-a-half-hour drive to the museum in Tres Zapotes, but it was worth it. Finally, I got a close-up look at one of the huge heads! I could not believe the details and wondered how the Olmec created such lifelike features. One of the museum experts said that the Olmec probably used handheld stone tools to carve the heads. The eyes, nose, and mouth looked so real. The giant heads are said to represent different Olmec rulers. The heads may have been used to honor the dead or mark different areas within the Olmec civilization.

How the Olmec carved such realistic features remains a mystery, but some historians believe they might have used wet reeds and sand to shape them.

Moving a Mountain

Next, I made my way to Cerro Cintepec in the Tuxtla Mountains. This was where the Olmec found the huge stone slabs they used to carve their heads. The heads ranged in height from about 5 to 11 feet (1.5 to 3.4 m) and weighed up to 8 tons (7.3 metric tons). The slabs they were made from must have been huge. The slabs were carried 50 miles (80 km) or more from the mountains. No one knows for sure how the Olmec did this. Historians **theorize** that they may have dragged the slabs down the side of the mountain, and then floated them along rivers on rafts. There must have been a lot of people involved!

Living in La Venta

My last stop was La Venta, where four Olmec heads have been found. I talked to an archaeologist working at La Venta. She told me that, so far, a total of 17 heads have been found, and each one is different. Mesoamericans believed a person's head contained their soul and emotions. Could that be why they only carved the head of each ruler and not their bodies?

Finding Answers

The Olmec heads were amazing, although details about how the slabs were transported and the heads were made remain a mystery. I kept a record of what I found—did you? Turn to pages 28–29 to learn if your findings match mine!

RULERS OF THE NORTH

Indigenous **peoples lived in present-day North America for thousands of years before Europeans arrived. Archaeologists have found evidence of Indigenous peoples that dates back at least 15,000 years. It includes firepits, burned bones, and stone tools. Over time, some Indigenous nations created empires that sprawled across the land. New evidence and artifacts are being discovered all the time that tell us more about North America's first people.**

Ancient Ones in America

The Ancestral Puebloans were Native Americans who ruled over the Southwest United States from about 100 C.E. They lived in present-day Arizona, New Mexico, Colorado, and Utah. They are known for their amazing farming skills, towering cliff dwellings, and sandstone **pueblos**. But by about 1300 C.E., the Ancestral Puebloans seemed to vanish without a trace. Historians do not know for sure what happened to them. Some believe they may have been killed by a drought or another group.

Riches of the Great White North

French explorers arrived in present-day Canada in the 1500s. There, they met Iroquoian and Algonquian people who spoke of a place with vast riches. The French called this place the Kingdom of Saguenay. For years, explorers searched for the Kingdom of Saguenay. It was said to lie north of the Saint Lawrence River, in what is now the province of Quebec. The explorers never found it. Did the Kingdom of Saguenay ever exist, and if so, where is it?

All that is left of the Ancestral Puebloans are their artifacts, such as this decorated jug.

Could a **Viking** settlement that was found at L'Anse aux Meadows on the island of Newfoundland be the Kingdom of Saguenay?

Mighty Mississippians

From 1000 C.E. until the arrival of Europeans in the mid-1500s, a mighty culture thrived across the present-day Midwest and Southeast United States. This Mississippian Empire was made up of several Native American **chiefdoms** that shared a similar way of life. Each had its own chief who governed over the land. Eventually, the empire collapsed—and to this day, historians are not sure why.

History Raider!

I remember seeing a display at a museum about the Mississippian Empire. I learned that Mississippian chiefdoms were known for the massive mounds of earth that dotted their lands. But how did they build these mounds, and how were they used? I had to find out more.

History Raider!

Mysterious Mounds

It was impossible to miss the massive mound of earth jutting toward the sky as I got closer to Cahokia Mounds State Historic Site in Collinsville, Illinois. This site is the remains of the massive Mississippian city Cahokia. It was only about a 15-minute drive from the city of St. Louis, Missouri, but it felt like a whole other world.

Climbing Monks Mound

At one time, there were 120 mounds at Cahokia. Today, around 70 mounds remain. Monks Mound is the largest of all the mounds. It stands about 100 feet (31 m) tall, and there are 154 steps to the top. That's a lot of steps!

Backbreaking Work

At the top, a researcher told me that the mounds had been built in stages over many years. Workers may have carried baskets of dirt on their backs, dumping them over and over to build the mound. Soil studies show that parts of Monks Mound were built using blocks of **sod** that had been turned upside down and stacked like bricks.

Mississippians probably lived in homes covered in a plaster made of mud and straw. The roof may have been made from grass thatch.

Monks Mound is one of just a few of the mounds at Cahokia that have been examined. There are more ancient secrets still waiting to be revealed.

Mound Puzzles

As I walked around the rest of the site, I learned that as many as 20,000 people once lived here. The mounds were used as a base for many buildings, houses, and temples. Monks Mound itself was home to a huge government building. Experts think the ruler may have lived at the top of the mound and held special ceremonies there. But what else were mounds used for? Could they have been used as grave sites, perhaps? Archaeologists found the remains of a man beneath one of the other mounds at Cahokia. They believe he was an important leader because he was surrounded by ornaments and arrows.

Finding Answers

I learned so much about the Mississippians by studying the mounds at Cahokia. Did you keep a note of the evidence you found? Turn to pages 28–29 to learn if your findings match mine!

ANCIENT AFRICA

As the birthplace of humankind, Africa has been home to countless civilizations since the beginning of human history. Many great African kings, queens, and kingdoms have seen their rise and fall across the continent since then. Today, scientists and historians are starting to discover these lost kingdoms and their histories.

Place of Power

In the mid-1500s, stories were told about a marvelous stone city in southern Africa. For centuries after, European explorers searched in earnest for the lost city, but never found it. Then, in the 1800s, the remains of a great city were found in central Zimbabwe. It was called Great Zimbabwe. Archaeologists believe the city was built by local people in medieval times. It was the capital of the wealthy Kingdom of Zimbabwe, which thrived from the 1000s to the 1400s. The city had remained hidden beneath the dust for years.

Egypt's Evil Queen?

Cleopatra was one of the most famous African rulers of all time. She was just 18 when her father died. She then took the throne, along with her 10-year-old brother, Ptolemy XIII. Cleopatra ruled Egypt for 21 years, from 51 to 30 B.C.E. Most of what we know about her comes from ancient writings of the Romans—and they disliked her. They said she won over Roman leaders to get them to do whatever she wanted. Some even thought she was a witch!

This portrait of Cleopatra is from the first century C.E. Today, it is on display at the National Archaeological Museum in Naples, Italy.

Love and War

Cleopatra had a relationship with Julius Caesar. He was a Roman **dictator** and one of the most powerful men in the world at the time. After Caesar was killed, Cleopatra began a romance with another Roman leader, Mark Antony.

Mark Antony was so taken by Cleopatra that he left his wife for her. On top of Cleopatra's love affairs, she is said to have had a hand in the deaths of three of her siblings. Ptolemy XIII died trying to escape from battle after Caesar helped Cleopatra raise an army to defeat him. She then ruled alongside another younger brother, Ptolemy XIV. Some say he was poisoned by Cleopatra. Finally, Antony had Cleopatra's sister killed at the queen's request to make sure she could never take away the throne.

Throughout the ages, images of Cleopatra have shown her as a beautiful woman. One of the most accurate images we have of her is on this coin, shown above left.

More than 2,000 years after her death, Cleopatra still captures the imaginations of people everywhere. Historians have pieced together the details of her life from ancient accounts and artifacts. But mysteries remain.

History Raider!

Could it be that Cleopatra really was as powerful as the history books say, or was there more to her story? What happened to the mysterious queen? And where does her tomb lie? I decided to investigate.

History Raider!

Deathly Mystery

My first stop was the Egyptian Museum in Cairo, Egypt. It featured a large collection of ancient Egyptian artifacts, including many from Cleopatra's time. I learned that there are very few **authentic** items that tell us about the queen. That's why most of our information is based on Roman writings about this famous ruler.

A Different Story

At the museum, one of the workers told me that a Greek historian named Plutarch wrote the most detailed account of Cleopatra's life. He said that everyone who met her found her charming and lovely. They thought that her wisdom was beautiful. Many other historic accounts say Cleopatra was educated in math, art, and other subjects. She spoke several languages. She built relationships with other countries and made Egypt wealthy. Some say she even wrote books on science, medicine, and other topics. She sounded so smart!

Sneaky Snake

I wanted to find out how Cleopatra died. Some modern stories say she died from a **self-inflicted** snakebite. Was this true? The worker said that snakebites are not always deadly, and it is an unlikely way to try to die. Cleopatra knew about poisons, however, so if she did die by suicide, that may have been what she used instead of a snake.

Lost Tomb

Some historians believe that Cleopatra's tomb was swept away by a giant wave that hit Alexandria in 365 C.E. and that it lies hidden beneath the waves to this day.

Where was Cleopatra buried, I wondered? I had heard a rumor that her tomb might be at the temple of Taposiris Magna. It is located 28 miles (45 km) west of Alexandria, the second-largest city in Egypt. I made my way there next. As I stood among the dusty ruins of the ancient temple, I learned that only a small portion of the area has been explored by archaeologists.

So far, they have found coins with Cleopatra's face, which links the queen to the area. There is also a statue of Antony and Cleopatra embracing. Other finds include the stone head from a statue of Cleopatra. But perhaps the most important find is two **mummies** covered in gold—one male and one female. Could they be Antony and Cleopatra? And could this indeed be her last resting place? Only time will tell.

Finding Answers

I still have questions about the long-lost queen's final resting place, but I did learn that Cleopatra was truly one of Africa's greatest rulers. I took lots of notes. How about you? Turn to pages 28–29 to see if your notes match mine!

ONGOING MYSTERIES

Discovering the secrets of great kingdoms that have been lost to history is exciting. And it is fascinating to imagine there may be many more ancient kingdoms just waiting to be discovered. Thanks to modern science, archaeologists have now found thousands of ancient sites. Modern equipment is helping unlock their mysteries.

Exploring Underground

Ground-penetrating radar (GPR) sends a pulse of energy into the ground. The pulse bounces back when it hits an object, such as a wall. A computer measures the time it takes for the pulse to bounce back. This tells archaeologists how deep the object is beneath the ground. Archaeologists can scan GPR over a large area to create a three-dimensional (3-D) map. They can then use the map to learn about the area without damaging the land or any objects beneath it.

This GPR machine allows the person using it to travel over an area and scan the ground beneath for lost treasures.

Today, archaeologists use **drones** like this one to study historical sites from high in the sky.

Searching from the Sky

Ancient buildings can leave a mark on Earth's surface long after they have been buried underground. They can even cause plants to grow in an unusual pattern. **Remote sensing** is a technique that archaeologists use to gather information about objects from a distance. Images from **satellites**, aircraft, or drones can be used to spot signs on the ground from overhead. This technique can uncover hundreds of ancient sites in a very short time.

History Raider!

For adventurers like us, the world is full of mysteries and wonders to explore. The world of great kings and kingdoms lost to history has been so much fun to explore, and journeys into the future look just as exciting!

MYSTERY SOLVED?

The stories behind the lost kingdoms and rulers are fascinating, aren't they? After gathering the evidence, here are some conclusions I made after each journey. How do yours match up?

Pages 8-9: Britain's Lost King

Although there is no actual proof that Arthur existed, artifacts found at Tintagel suggest that important and wealthy people lived there. Arthur may have been one of them. Caerleon, Wales, could very well have been the site of Camelot. The bones of Arthur and his wife were thought to have been buried in Glastonbury Abbey, but they were destroyed in a fire.

Pages 12-13: Temple Lost in Time

The temple was built by Hindus, which explains why it has carvings of Hindu gods. The temple was built in the 12th century, long after Mouhout claimed it was built. After a period of drought, there were vast floods, which probably washed away much of the great city.

Pages 16-17: Losing Their Heads

The heads are made from stone from the Tuxla Mountains. Each of the heads is very detailed and has unique features. They were most likely carved by handheld tools. Each is said to represent a different Olmec leader.

Pages 20-21: Mysterious Mounds

The mounds were most likely made by pouring baskets of dirt onto the site. They were probably the foundation for important buildings, such as government offices and temples. Remains of a person have been found in one mound, so they may also have been grave sites.

Pages 24-25: Deathly Mystery

Cleopatra was a smart, strong woman. She was well educated and improved Egypt's wealth. She is believed to have died a quick and painless death, most likely from poison. No one has found her tomb, but it may lie under the sea near Alexandria or at the temple of Taposiris Magna.

GLOSSARY

abbey A building where nuns or monks live

amphitheater An oval-shaped arena

archaeologists People who study history through artifacts and remains

artifacts Objects that were made by people in the past

authentic Something that is factual

chiefdoms Areas ruled by chiefs

civilizations Settled and organized groups of people

culture A society that has its own beliefs, art, and way of life

dictator A ruler who has total control

DNA The substance in cells that carries unique information about living things

drones Unmanned aircraft

drought A long period with little or no rainfall

empire A group of states or countries ruled over by a single person

evidence A sign that shows that something exists or is true

excavating Digging or removing earth

fortification A structure built to protect an area against enemy attack

ground-penetrating radar (GPR) A device that uses radar pulses to detect objects under the earth

historians People who study history

Indigenous Describes people who lived naturally in a particular area

Latin America The countries of South America, plus Mexico, Central America, and the Caribbean islands

medieval Describes the time between 500 and 1500 C.E.

Mesoamerica An area that stretched from central Mexico to Honduras and Nicaragua

monks Men dedicated to religion

mummies Bodies that are preserved

pueblos Multistory stone settlements

remains Pieces or parts of something that are left when most of it has been used up or destroyed

remote sensing Scanning objects from a distance to gather information

satellites Machines in space that move around objects to collect information

self-inflicted Caused harm to oneself

sod A piece of grass and soil

theorize To form an idea about how something happened

tomb A place where a person is buried

tribe Group that has a common religion, culture, and beliefs

Viking A Scandinavian who lived from the 800s to the 1000s

LEARNING MORE

BOOKS

Rodger, Ellen. *Ancient Egypt Inside Out* (Ancient Worlds Inside Out). Crabtree Publishing, 2017.

Van Vleet, Carmella. *Ancient Civilizations: Romans!* (Explore Your World). Nomad Press, 2019.

Waldron, Melanie. *Geography Matters in the Inca Empire* (Geography Matters in Ancient Civilizations). Heinemann, 2015.

Williams, Marcia. *The Romans: Gods, Emperors, and Dormice.* Candlewick, 2018.

WEBSITES

Find out more about Mississippian mounds at:
https://cahokiamounds.org/learn

Explore the ancient history of Machu Picchu at:
https://worldoftravelswithkids.com/machu-picchu-facts-for-kids

Learn about the legend of King Arthur at:
https://kids.britannica.com/kids/article/King-Arthur/543478

Uncover the secrets of Angkor at:
https://whc.unesco.org/en/list/668

About the Author

Heather C. Hudak has written hundreds of books on all kinds of topics. When she is not writing, Heather loves to travel all over the world. She enjoys visiting ancient sites and piecing together clues about what happened to the people who once lived there. Like Madison Maverick, Heather has watched the sunrise at Angkor Wat, explored the ancient ruins of the Roman Empire, and climbed the stone steps of a once-hidden Mayan temple in Mexico.